The Customs of the
Kingdoms of India

The Indian Ocean, *c*. 1310

MARCO POLO

The Customs of the
Kingdoms of India

Translated by RONALD LATHAM

GREAT
JOURNEYS

PENGUIN BOOKS

Published by the Penguin Group
Penguin Books Ltd, 80 Strand, London WC2R 0RL, England
Penguin Group (USA) Inc., 375 Hudson Street, New York, New York 10014, USA
Penguin Group (Canada), 90 Eglinton Avenue East, Suite 700, Toronto, Ontario, Canada M4P 2Y3
(a division of Pearson Penguin Canada Inc.)
Penguin Ireland, 25 St Stephen's Green, Dublin 2, Ireland (a division of Penguin Books Ltd)
Penguin Group (Australia), 250 Camberwell Road, Camberwell, Victoria 3124, Australia
(a division of Pearson Australia Group Pty Ltd)
Penguin Books India Pvt Ltd, 11 Community Centre, Panchsheel Park, New Delhi – 110 017, India
Penguin Group (NZ), 67 Apollo Drive, Rosedale, North Shore 0632, New Zealand
(a division of Pearson New Zealand Ltd)
Penguin Books (South Africa) (Pty) Ltd, 24 Sturdee Avenue, Rosebank, Johannesburg 2196, South Africa

Penguin Books Ltd, Registered Offices: 80 Strand, London WC2R 0RL, England

www.penguin.com

This translation first published as *The Travels* in Penguin Books 1958
This extract published in Penguin Books 2007
2

Translation copyright © Ronald Latham, 1958
All rights reserved

Inside-cover maps by Jeff Edwards

Typeset by Rowland Phototypesetting Ltd, Bury St Edmunds, Suffolk
Printed in England by Clays Ltd, St Ives plc

ISBN: 978-0-141-03203-0

Contents

Marco Polo (1254–1324), a Venetian merchant, spent many years in the service of Kubilai Khan and in his journeys to and from the Khan's court and around the Mongol Empire picked up immense amounts of direct and indirect knowledge about Asia. After his return to Europe he became involved in fighting between Venice and Genoa, was made a prisoner-of-war and in prison met Rustichello da Pisa, who wrote down the story of Polo's adventures.

This selection recounts Polo's knowledge of the countries around the Indian Ocean – a hectic blend of correct, careful information and the wildest fantasy. It will never be established just what Polo saw himself and where he actually went, but his work introduced Europeans to a world which was almost entirely barred to them and it profoundly influenced centuries of exploration and imagination.

Hormuz, Persia and the Land of the Assassins

Here on the coast stands a city called Hormuz, which has an excellent harbour. Merchants come here by ship from India, bringing all sorts of spices and precious stones and pearls and cloths of silk and of gold and elephants' tusks and many other wares. In this city they sell them to others, who distribute them to various customers through the length and breadth of the world. It is a great centre of commerce, with many cities and towns subordinate to it, and the capital of the kingdom. Its king is named Ruemedan Ahmad. The climate is torrid, owing to the heat of the sun, and unhealthy. If a merchant dies here, the king confiscates all his possessions.

In this country they make date wine with the addition of various spices, and very good it is. When it is drunk by men who are not used to it, it loosens the bowels and makes a thorough purge; but after that it does them good and makes them put on flesh. The natives do not eat our sort of food, because a diet of wheaten bread and meat would make them ill. To keep well they eat dates and salt fish, that is, tunny, and also onions; and on this diet they thrive.

Their ships are very bad, and many of them founder, because they are not fastened with iron nails but stitched together with thread made of coconut husks.

They soak the husk till it assumes the texture of horse-hair; then they make it into threads and stitch their ships. It is not spoilt by the salt water, but lasts remarkably well. The ships have one mast, one sail, and one rudder and are not decked; when they have loaded them, they cover the cargo with skins, and on top of these they put the horses which they ship to India for sale. They have no iron for nails; so they employ wooden pegs and stitch with thread. This makes it a risky undertaking to sail in these ships. And you can take my word that many of them sink, because the Indian Ocean is often very stormy.

The people here are black and worship Mahomet. In summer they do not stay in the cities, or they would all die of the heat; but they go out to their gardens, where there are rivers and sheets of water. Here they build arbours of hurdles, resting at one end on the bank and at the other on piles driven in below the water, and covered with foliage to fend off the sun. Even so, they would not escape, were it not for one thing of which I will tell you. It is a fact that several times in the summer there comes a wind from the direction of the sandy wastes that lie around this plain, a wind so overpoweringly hot that it would be deadly if it did not happen that, as soon as men are aware of its approach, they plunge neck-deep into the water and so escape from the heat. To show just how hot this wind can be, Messer Marco gives the following account of something that happened when he was in these parts. The king of Kerman, not having received the tribute due to him from the lord of Hormuz, resolved to seize his opportunity when the men of Hormuz were living outside the city in the open. He accordingly mustered 1,600 horse and 5,000 foot-soldiers and sent them across the plain of Rudbar to make a surprise attack. One day, having failed through faulty guidance to reach the place appointed for the night's halt, they bivouacked in a wood not far from Hormuz. Next morning, when they were on the point of setting out, the hot wind came down on them and stifled them all, so that not one survived to carry back the news to their lord. The men of Hormuz, hearing of this, went out to bury the corpses, so that they should not infect the air. When they gripped them by the arms to drag them to the graves, they were so parched by the tremendous heat that the arms came loose from the trunk, so that there was nothing for it but to dig the graves beside the corpses and heave them in.

In this district they sow their wheat and barley and other grains in November, and they have got in all their harvest before the end of March. And so with all their fruits: by March they are ripened and done with. After that you will find no vegetation anywhere except date-palms, which last till May. This is due to the great heat, which withers up everything.

Another feature of the ships here is that they are not caulked with pitch but anointed with a sort of fish oil.

Let me tell you next that when a man has died here, or a woman, they make a great to-do about mourning. Gentlewomen mourn their dead fully four years after death, at least once a day. They assemble with their kinsfolk and neighbours and give themselves up to loud wailing and keening and lamenting the dead. Since deaths are frequent, they are never done with mourning. There are even women among them who specialize in lamentation and are daily on hire to bewail the lost ones of other men and women.

So much for this city. We shall not touch on India at this point; for I will deal with it later at the appropriate time and place. Now I will turn back towards the north to speak of the countries in that quarter. We shall return by another route to the city of Kerman of which I have spoken, because there is no way of going to these countries except from this city. And you must understand that king Ruemedan Ahmad, whom we have just left, is a vassal of the king of Kerman.

The return journey from Hormuz to Kerman passes through a fine plain amply stocked with foodstuffs. It is blessed with natural hot baths. Partridges are plentiful and very cheap. Fruit trees and date-palms abound. The wheaten bread here is so bitter that no one can eat it unless he is accustomed to it. This is due to the bitterness of the water. The baths, of which I have spoken above, are formed from springs of very hot water; they are good for many ailments, especially affections of the skin.

Now let me start my account of the countries lying to the north. When the traveller leaves Kerman, he rides for seven days along a very uninviting road through wild and barren country. I will tell you what it is like. For three days he finds no running water, or as good as none. What water there is is brackish and green as meadow grass and so bitter that no one could bear to drink it. Drink one drop of it and you void your bowels ten times over. It is the same with the salt that is made from it: if you eat one little granule, it produces violent diarrhoea. So the men who travel this way carry water with them to drink. Animals will drink the brackish water under stress of extreme thirst, and you may take my word that it afflicts them violently with diarrhoea. And in all these three days' journey there is no habitation; it is all a desolate and arid waste. There are no beasts at all, because they could find nothing to eat.

At the end of this time the traveller arrives at a stream of fresh water which runs underground. In certain places there are caverns carved and scooped out by the action of the stream; through these it can be seen to flow, and then suddenly it plunges underground. Nevertheless, there is abundance of water, by whose banks wayfarers wearied by the hardships of the desert behind them may rest and refresh themselves with their beasts.

Then begins another stretch of four days' duration, just as desolate and arid, where the water is just as bitter and there are no trees or beasts, excepting only asses. At the end of this stretch we leave the kingdom of Kerman and reach the city of Kuh-banan.

This is a large city. Its inhabitants worship Mahomet. There is iron and steel and *ondanique* in plenty, and they make steel mirrors of large size and excellent quality. They also make *tutty*, which is a very good salve for the eyes, and *spodium*. Let me explain how they do it. They take a vein of earth that is suited for the purpose and heap it in a furnace with a blazing fire, above which is an iron grid. The fumes and vapour given off by this earth and trapped by the grid constitute *tutty*; the residue remaining in the fire is *spodium*. Now let us continue our journey.

When the traveller leaves Kuh-banan he goes for fully eight days through a desert in which there is utter drought and neither fruit nor trees and where the water is as bitter and as bad as before. He is obliged to carry with him all that he needs to eat and drink, except the water that the beasts drink very reluctantly – they may be tempted to drink by mixing flour with it. After these eight days he reaches a province called Tun and Kain, where there are cities and towns in plenty. It is situated on the northern borders of Persia. There is an immense plain here, in which stands the Solitary Tree, which the Christians call the Dry Tree. Let me describe it to you. It is of great size and girth. Its leaves are green on one side, white on the other. It produces husks like chestnut husks; but there is nothing in them. Its wood is hard and yellow like box-wood. And there are no trees near it for more than 100 miles, except in one direction where there are trees ten miles away. It is here, according to the people of the country, that the battle was fought between Alexander and Darius. The villages and towns hereabouts enjoy great abundance of good things of every sort; for the climate is admirably tempered, neither too hot nor too cold. The people all worship Mahomet. They are a good-looking race and the women in particular are of outstanding beauty.

Now let us proceed farther, and I will tell you about a country called Mulehet.

Mulehet, which means 'heretics' according to the law of the Saracens, is the country where the Sheikh of the Mountain used to live in days gone by. I will tell you his story just as I, Messer Marco, have heard it told by many people.

The Sheikh was called in their language Alaodin. He had had made in a valley between two mountains the biggest and most beautiful garden that was ever seen, planted with all the finest fruits in the world and containing the most splendid mansions and palaces that were ever seen, ornamented with gold and with likenesses of all that is beautiful on earth, and also four conduits, one flowing with wine, one with milk, one with honey, and one with water. There were fair ladies there and damsels, the loveliest in the world, unrivalled at playing every sort of instrument and at singing and dancing. And he gave his men to understand that this garden was Paradise. That is why he had made it after this pattern, because Mahomet assured the Saracens that those who go to Paradise will have beautiful women to their hearts' content to do their bidding, and will find there rivers of wine and milk and honey and water. So he had had this garden made like the Paradise that Mahomet promised to the Saracens, and the Saracens of this country believed that it really was Paradise. No one ever entered the garden except those whom he wished to make Assassins. At the entrance stood a castle so strong that it need fear no man in the world,

7

and there was no other way in except through this castle. The Sheikh kept with him at his court all the youths of the country from twelve years old to twenty, all, that is, who shaped well as men at arms. These youths knew well by hearsay that Mahomet their prophet had declared Paradise to be made of such a fashion as I have described, and so they accepted it as truth. Now mark what follows. He used to put some of these youths in this Paradise, four at a time, or ten, or twenty, according as he wished. And this is how he did it. He would give them draughts that sent them to sleep on the spot. Then he had them taken and put in the garden, where they were wakened. When they awoke and found themselves in there and saw all the things I have told you of, they believed they were really in Paradise. And the ladies and damsels stayed with them all the time, singing and making music for their delight and ministering to all their desires. So these youths had all they could wish for and asked nothing better than to remain there.

Now the Sheikh held his court with great splendour and magnificence and bore himself most nobly and convinced the simple mountain folk round about that he was a prophet; and they believed it to be the truth. And when he wanted emissaries to send on some mission of murder, he would administer the drug to as many as he pleased; and while they slept he had them carried into his palace. When these youths awoke and found themselves in the castle within the palace, they were amazed and by no means glad, for the Paradise from which they had come was not a place that they

8

would ever willingly have left. They went forthwith to the Sheikh and humbled themselves before him, as men who believed that he was a great prophet. When he asked them whence they came, they would answer that they came from Paradise, and that this was in truth the Paradise of which Mahomet had told their ancestors; and they would tell their listeners all that they had found there. And the others who heard this and had not been there were filled with a great longing to go to this Paradise; they longed for death so that they might go there, and looked forward eagerly to the day of their going.

When the Sheikh desired the death of some great lord, he would first try an experiment to find out which of his Assassins were the best. He would send some off on a mission in the neighbourhood at no great distance with orders to kill such and such a man. They went without demur and did the bidding of their lord. Then, when they had killed the man, they returned to court – those of them that escaped, for some were caught and put to death. When they had returned to their lord and told him that they had faithfully performed their task, the Sheikh would make a great feast in their honour. And he knew very well which of them had displayed the greatest zeal, because after each he had sent others of his men as spies to report which was the most daring and the best hand at murdering. Then, in order to bring about the death of the lord or other man which he desired, he would take some of these Assassins of his and send them wherever he might wish, telling them that he was minded to dispatch them to Paradise: they were to go accordingly and kill such and such a man; if they died on their mission, they would go there all the sooner. Those who received such a command obeyed it with a right good will, more readily than anything else they might have been called on to do. Away they went and did all that they were commanded. Thus it happened that no one ever escaped when the Sheikh of the Mountain desired his death. And I can assure you that many kings and many lords paid tribute to him and cultivated his friendship for fear that he might bring about their death. This happened because at that time the nations were not united in their allegiance, but torn by conflicting loyalties and purposes.

I have told you about the Sheikh of the Mountain and his Assassins. Now let me tell you how he was overthrown and by whom. But first I will tell you something else about him that I had omitted. You must know that this Sheikh had chosen as his subordinates two other Sheikhs, who adopted all his practices and customs. One of these he dispatched to the neighbourhood of Damascus, the other to Kurdistan. Let us now turn to the subject of his overthrow. It happened about the year of Our Lord's nativity 1262 that Hulagu, lord of the Tartars of the Levant, knowing of all the evil deeds this Sheikh was doing, made up his mind that he should be crushed. So he appointed some of his barons and sent them against this castle with a powerful force. For fully three years they besieged the castle without being able to take it. Indeed they never would have taken it so long as the besieged had anything to eat, but at the end of the three years they had no food left. So they were taken, and the Sheikh, Alaodin, was put to death with all his men. And from that time to this there have been no more of these Sheikhs and no more Assassins; but with him there came an end to all the power that had been wielded of old by the Sheikhs of the Mountain and all the evil they had done.

Ceylon and the Islands of the Bay of Bengal

When the traveller leaves Lesser Java and the kingdom of Lambri and sails northwards for about 150 miles, he reaches two islands, one of which is called Nicobar. In this island there is no king, and the people live like beasts. I assure you that they go stark naked, men and women alike, without any covering of any sort. They are idolaters. They have very beautiful cloths or sashes some three fathoms in length, made of silk of every colour. They buy them from passing traders and keep them hung over rails in their houses as a token of wealth and magnificence, just as we keep pearls and precious stones and vessels of gold and silver. They make no use of them whatsoever, but keep them only for show. And whoever has most of them, and of the greatest beauty, is esteemed as the greatest and most honourable. All the forests in this island are of noble trees of great worth: these are red sandal, coconuts (which among us are called Pharaoh's nuts), apples of paradise, cloves, brazil, and many other good trees. As there is nothing else worth mentioning, we shall pass on and tell you of the other island, whose name is Andaman.

Andaman is a very big island. The people have no king. They are idolaters and live like wild beasts. Now let me tell you of a race of men well worth describing in our book. You may take it for a fact that all the men of this island have heads like dogs, and teeth and eyes like dogs; for I assure you that the whole aspect of their faces is that of big mastiffs. They are a very cruel race: whenever they can get hold of a man who is not one of their kind, they devour him. They have abundance of spices of every kind. Their food is rice and milk, and every sort of flesh. They also have coconuts, apples of paradise, and many other fruit different from ours. The island lies in a sea so turbulent and so deep that ships cannot anchor there or sail away from it, because it sweeps them into a gulf from which they can never escape. This is because the sea there is so tempestuous that it is continually eating away the land, scooping out trees at the root and toppling them over and afterwards sweeping them into this gulf. It is truly marvellous how many trees are driven into the gulf without ever coming out again. Hence it happens that ships that enter the gulf are jammed in such a mass of these trees that they cannot move from the spot and so are stuck there for good.

On leaving the island of Andaman and sailing for 1,000 miles a little south of west, the traveller reaches Ceylon, which is undoubtedly the finest island of its size in all the world. Let me explain how. It has a circumference of some 2,400 miles. And I assure you that it used to be bigger than this. For it was once as much as 3,500 miles, as appears in the mariners' charts of this sea. But the north wind blows so strongly in these parts that it has submerged a great part of this island under the sea. That is why it is no longer as big as it used to be.

Now I will tell you something about the island. It is ruled by a king called Sendernam. The people are idolaters. They pay no tribute to anyone. They go quite naked, except that they cover their private parts. They have no grain other than rice. They have sesame, from which they make oil. They live on milk, flesh and rice, and have wine made from trees such as I have described above. They have abundance of brazil, the best in the world. Let me add that they have also the most precious thing to be found anywhere in the world; for in this island, and nowhere else in the world, are produced superb and authentic rubies. The island also produces sapphires, topazes, amethysts, garnets, and many other precious stones. And I assure you that the king of this province possesses the finest ruby that exists in all the world – the finest certainly, that was ever seen or is ever likely to be seen. Let me describe it to you. It is about a palm in length and of the thickness of a man's arm. It is the most brilliant object to behold in all the world, free from any flaw and glowing red like fire. It is so precious that it could scarcely be bought for money. I tell you in all truthfulness that the Great Khan sent emissaries to this king and told him that he wished to buy this ruby and that if he would part with it he would give him the value of a city. But the king declared that he would not part with it for anything in the world, because it was an heirloom from his ancestors. For this reason the Khan could not have it at any price.

The inhabitants of Ceylon are not fighting men, but

paltry and mean-spirited creatures. If they have need of the services of soldiers, they hire them from abroad, especially Saracens. Since there is nothing else here worth mentioning, we shall now pass on to India.

The Kingdoms of the Coromandel and Malabar Coast

When the traveller leaves Ceylon and sails westwards for about sixty miles, he arrives in the great province of Maabar, which is called Greater India. It is indeed the best part of India. This province forms part of the mainland. It is ruled by five kings, who are all brothers by birth; and we will tell you of each one separately. You may take it for a fact that it is the richest and most splendid province in the world; and I will tell you how.

The foremost kingdom of the province is ruled by one of these brothers, whose name is Sender Bandi Devar. In his kingdom are found pearls of great size and beauty; for you must know that Maabar and Ceylon between them produce most of the pearls and gems that are to be found in the world. I will tell you how these pearls are found and gathered.

You must understand that in this sea is a gulf between the island and the mainland; and in all this gulf there is no more than eight or ten fathoms of water and in some places no more than two. It is in this gulf that the pearls are gathered; and I will tell you how. A group of merchants will band together to form a company or partnership and will take a large ship specially adapted for the purpose, in which each will have a handy cabin fitted for his use containing a tub of water and other requisites. There will be a great

16

many such ships, because there are many merchants who devote themselves to this sort of fishery. And all the merchants who are associated in one ship will have several boats to tow her through the gulf. It is their practice to hire men for a certain sum for the month of April and half of May; for that is the fishing season in this gulf. The place where pearls are most plentiful is called Bettala, and is on the mainland. From there they sail out for sixty miles towards the south and there cast anchor. Then they go out in the little boats and begin to fish in a manner that I will describe to you. The men in the little boats, who have been hired by the merchants, jump overboard and dive into the water, sometimes three fathoms down, sometimes four, sometimes as much as ten. They stay under as long as they can. When they can endure no longer, they come to the surface, rest a short while and then plunge in again; and so they continue all day. While they are at the bottom of the sea, they gather there certain shells which are called sea oysters. In these oysters are found pearls, big and small and of every variety. The shells are split open and put into the tubs of water of which I have spoken. The pearls are embedded in the flesh of the shellfish. In the water this flesh decays and grows flabby and takes on the appearance of white of egg. In this form it floats to the surface, while the pearls divested of impurities remain at the bottom. That is how the pearls are gathered. And I assure you that the quantities obtained are beyond computation. For you must know that pearls gathered in this gulf are exported throughout the world, because most of them are round and lustrous. In the middle of May this fishing comes to a stop, because the pearl-bearing shells are no longer to be found. But it is a fact that about 300 miles away they are found in September and the earlier half of October.

I can assure you that the king of this kingdom derives an immense revenue from the duty paid on this fishery. For the merchants pay him a tithe of their takings. Over and above this they pay one pearl in twenty to men who protect the divers against predatory fish by means of incantations. These enchanters are called Brahmans. They utter their incantations by day only; at night they break off their spells, so that the fish are free to do as they please. These Brahmans are expert also in incantations against all sorts of beasts and birds and animals of every kind.

I must tell you that in all this province of Maabar there is no master tailor or dressmaker to cut or stitch cloth, because the people go stark naked all the year round. For the weather here is always temperate, that is, it is neither cold nor hot. That is why they always go naked, except that they cover their private parts with a scrap of cloth. The king wears no more than the others, apart from certain ornaments of which I will tell you. You may take it for a fact that he too goes stark naked, except for a handsome loin-cloth with a fringe all round it set with precious stones – rubies, sapphires, emeralds, and other brilliant gems – so that this scrap of cloth is worth a fortune. Slung round his neck is a cord of fine silk which hangs down a full pace in front of him, and strung on this necklace are 104 beads, consisting of large and beautiful pearls and rubies of immense value. Let me tell you why he wears this necklace. He does it because it is his task every day, morning and evening, to say 104 prayers in honour of his idols. Such is the bidding of their faith and their religion, and such was the wont of the kings who preceded him, which they left as an obligation incumbent on their successor. That is why the king wears these 104 beads round his neck. The prayer consists simply of the word '*Pacauta, Pacauta, Pacauta*' and nothing more. He also wears, in three places on his arm, bracelets of gold studded with precious stones and pearls of great size and value. In like manner he wears, in three places on his legs, three anklets adorned with costly pearls and gems. Let me tell you further that this same king wears on his toes splendid pearls and other jewels, so that it is a marvellous sight to behold. What need of more words? Suffice it that he wears in all so many gems and pearls that their price exceeds that of a fine city. Indeed no one could compute the total cost of all the jewellery he wears. And it is no wonder he wears so many, considering that all these pearls and gems are found in his own kingdom.

Let me tell you something else. No one is allowed to take out of his kingdom any large or costly gem or any pearl that weighs upwards of half a *saggio*. Several times a year throughout his reign he issues a proclamation that all who have pearls or gems of especial beauty and excellence shall bring them to his court, and he will give in return twice their value. It is the custom of the realm to pay double value for all gems of high quality. So merchants and any others who possess such stones are willing enough to take them to the court, because they are well paid. That is how it comes about that this king has such riches and so many precious stones.

Let me tell you next of some other marvels. First, you may take it for a fact that this king has fully 500 wives, that is concubines. For I assure you that, whenever he sets eye on a beautiful woman or damsel, he takes her for himself. This involved him on one occasion in an act of folly, as you shall hear. He coveted a beautiful woman who was his brother's wife and ravished her from him and kept her for himself. And his brother, who was a wise man, submitted in peace and did not quarrel with him. More than once he was on the point of making war on him, but their mother showed them her breasts, saying: 'If you fight with each other, I will cut off these breasts which gave you both suck.' And so the grievance was allowed to lapse.

Here is another thing at which you may well marvel. I assure you that this king has no lack of loyal henchmen of an unusual kind; for they are his henchmen in this world and the next, according to their own assertions. These henchmen attend upon the king in court; they go out riding with him; they enjoy places of great dignity in his service; wherever he goes, these barons bear him company and they exercise high authority throughout the kingdom. Then, when the king dies and his body is burning on a huge pyre, all these barons who were his henchmen, as I have told you, fling themselves into the fire and burn with the king in order to bear him company in the next world.

Here is another custom that prevails in this kingdom. When the king dies and leaves behind him a great treasure, the son who inherits would not touch it for anything in the world. For he says: 'I have all my father's kingdom and all his people; so I am well able to provide for myself as he did.' Hence the kings of this kingdom never touch their treasure, but hand it down from one to another, each accumulating his own hoard. For this reason the total accumulation is truly immense.

Let me tell you next that this country does not breed horses. Hence all the annual revenue, or the greater part of it, is spent in the purchase of horses; and I will tell you how. You may take it for a fact that the merchants of Hormuz and Kais, of Dhofar and Shihr and Aden, all of which provinces produce large numbers of battle chargers and other horses, buy up the best horses and load them on ships and export them to this king and his four brother kings. Some of them are sold for as much as 500 *saggi* of gold, which are worth more than 100 marks of silver. And I assure you that this king buys 2,000 of them and more every year, and his brothers as many. And by the end of the year not 100 of them survive. They all die through ill usage, because they have no veterinaries and do not know how to treat them. You may take it from me that the merchants who export them do not send out any veterinaries or allow any to go, because they are only too glad for many of them to die in the king's charge.

Another custom of the realm is this. When a man is guilty of a capital offence and the king has decreed his death, the offender declares that he wishes to kill himself out of respect and devotion to some particular idol. The king expresses his approval. Then all the offender's kinsfolk and friends take him and set him on a chair and give him fully a dozen swords and carry him through the city, proclaiming aloud: 'This brave man is going to kill himself for love of such-and-such an idol.' In this way they carry him through the whole city. When they have reached the place where justice is done, then the offender takes a knife and cries in a loud voice: 'I kill myself for love of such-and-such an idol.' Having spoken these words, he takes two swords and thrusts them into his thighs at one stroke. Then, he thrusts two into his arms, two into his belly, two into his chest. And so he thrusts them all in, crying aloud at each stroke: 'I kill myself for love of such-and-such an idol.' When they are all thrust in, then grasping a two-handled knife like those used for shaping hoops, he sets it against his nape, gives it a mighty pull and severs his own neck, because the knife is exceedingly sharp. After he has killed himself, his kinsfolk cremate the body amid great rejoicing.

Another custom is this. When a man is dead and his body is being cremated, his wife flings herself into the same fire and lets herself be burnt with her husband. The ladies who do this are highly praised by all. And I assure you that there are many who do as I have told you.

The people of this kingdom worship idols. Most of them worship the ox, because they say that it is a very good thing. No one would eat beef for anything in the world, and no one would kill an ox on any account. There is one race of men here called *gavi*, who eat beef. They do not indeed venture to slaughter cattle; but when an ox dies naturally or by some other mode of death, then these *gavi* eat it. Let me tell you further that they daub all their houses with cow-dung.

Here is yet another of their customs. The king and his barons and everyone else all sit on the earth. If you ask them why they do not seat themselves more honourably, they reply that to sit on the earth is honourable enough, because we were made from the earth and to the earth we must return, so that no one could honour the earth too highly and no one should slight it.

Let me tell you further that these *gavi* – that is, all the race of those that eat cattle when they die a natural death – are the same who in the old days slew Messer St Thomas the Apostle. And let me add that of all this tribe called *gavi* no one may enter the place where the body of Messer St Thomas lies. For you must know that ten men would not avail to hold one of these *gavi* in the place, nor could twenty or more bring one of them where the body lies; for the place will not receive them, by virtue of the holy body.

This kingdom produces no grain excepting only rice. And here is a greater matter, well worth recounting: in this country if a stallion of noble breed covers a mare of the like mettle, the offspring is a stunted colt with its feet awry. Horses so bred are worthless and cannot be ridden.

The people here go into battle with lance and shield and they go stark naked. They are not men of any valour or spirit, but paltry creatures and mean-spirited. They kill no beasts or any living thing. When they have a mind to eat the flesh of a sheep or of any beast or bird, they employ a Saracen or some other who is not of their religion or rule to kill it for them. Another of their customs is that all of them, male and female, wash their whole body in cold water twice a day – that is, morning and evening. One who did not wash twice a day would be thought an ascetic, as we think of the Patarins.

And you must know that in eating they use only the right hand; they would never touch food with their left. Whatever is clean and fair they do and touch with the right hand, believing that the function of the left hand is confined to such needful tasks as are unclean and foul, such as wiping the nose or the breach and suchlike. Likewise they drink only out of flasks, each one from his own; for no one would drink out of another's flask. When they are drinking, they do not set the flask to their lips, but hold it above and pour the fluid into their mouth. They would not on any account touch the flask with their lips nor pass it to a stranger to drink out of. If a stranger wants to drink and has not got his own flask with him, they will pour the wine or other fluid into his hands and he will drink out of them, so that his own hands will serve him for a cup.

I assure you that in this kingdom justice is very

strictly administered to those who commit homicide or theft or any other crime. Concerning debts the following rule and enactment is observed among them. If a debtor after many demands from his creditor for repayment of a debt continues day after day to put him off with promises, and if the creditor can get at him in such a way as to draw a circle round him, the debtor must not move out of the circle without first satisfying the creditor or giving firm and adequate surety for full repayment on the same day. Otherwise, if he should venture to leave the circle without payment or surety given, he would incur the penalty of death as an offender against the right and justice established by the ruler. And Messer Marco saw this done in the case of the king himself. For it happened that the king was indebted to a certain foreign merchant for some goods that he had had of him, and after many requests from the merchant repeatedly postponed repayment to save himself trouble. Then the merchant, because this delay seriously hampered him in his business, went up to the king one day when he was riding in the country and having made due preparation drew a circle round him, horse and all, on the earth. When the king saw this, he reined in his horse and did not move from the spot till the merchant had been satisfied in full. At sight of this the people standing round about exclaimed in admiration: 'See how the king has obeyed the rule of justice!' And the king replied: 'Shall I, who have established this rule, break it merely because it tells against me? Surely it is incumbent on me before all others to observe it.'

Most of the people here abstain from drinking wine. They will not admit as a witness or a guarantor either a wine-drinker or one who sails on the sea. For they say that a man who goes to sea must be a man in despair. On the other hand you should know that they do not regard any form of sexual indulgence as a sin.

The climate is amazingly hot, which explains why they go naked. There is no rain except in the months of June, July, and August. If it were not for the rain in these three months, which freshens the air, the heat would be so oppressive that no one could stand it. But thanks to this rain the heat is tempered.

Among these people there are many experts in the art called physiognomy, that is, the recognition of the characters of men and women, whether they be good or bad. This is done merely by looking at the man or woman. They are expert too in the significance of encounters with birds or beasts, and they pay more attention to augury than any other people in the world and are more skilled in distinguishing good omens from bad. I assure you that, when a man is setting out on a journey and happens to hear someone else sneeze, he promptly sits down by the way and goes no farther; if the other sneezes a second time, he gets up and goes ahead; if not, he turns back from the journey on which he has started and goes home.

Likewise they say that for every day in the week there is one unlucky hour, which they call *choiach*. Thus on Monday it is the hour after seven in the morning, on Tuesday after nine, on Wednesday the first hour after noon, and so forth throughout the year. All these they have written down and defined in their books. They tell the hour by measuring the height of a man's shadow in feet. Thus on such-and-such a day, when a man's shadow is seven feet long opposite the sun, then will be the hour of *choiach*. When it has passed this length either in increase or decrease – for as the sun rises the shadow shortens, as the sun drops it lengthens – then it is no longer *choiach*. On another day, when the shadow is twelve feet long, then will be *choiach*; and when this measure is passed, then *choiach* will be over. All this they have in writing. And you must know that in these hours they fight shy of making a bargain or doing any sort of business. While two men are in the act of bargaining together, some one will stand up in the sunlight and measure the shadow; and if it is within the limits of the forbidden hour, according to which day it may be, then he will immediately say to them: 'It is *choiach*. Do nothing.' And they will give over. Then he will measure a second time and finding that the hour is past will say to them: '*Choiach* is over. Do what you will.' And they have this sort of computation at their finger tips. For they say that, if anyone strikes a bargain in these hours, he will make no profit by it, but it will turn out badly for him.

Again, their houses are infested with certain animals called tarantulas, which run up the walls like lizards. They have a poisonous bite and do serious harm to a man if they bite him. They have an utterance as if they were saying '*chis!*' and this is the noise they make. These tarantulas are taken as an omen in the following way: when men are bargaining together in a house infested with these creatures and a tarantula utters its cry above them, they take note from which side of the bargainer, either purchaser or vendor, the cry emanates – whether left or right, before or behind or directly overhead – and according to the direction they know whether its significance is good or bad. If it is good, the bargain is struck; if bad, it is called off. Sometimes it is good for the vendor and bad for the purchaser or conversely, or for both or neither; and they guide their conduct accordingly. This lore is based on experience.

In this kingdom as soon as a child is born, whether boy or girl, the father and mother have a record made in writing of his nativity, that is, the day of his birth, the month, the lunar cycle and the hour. This they do because they guide all their actions by the counsel of astrologers and diviners who are skilled in enchantment and magic and geomancy.

Again, a man who has sons here turns them out of the house as soon as they reach the age of thirteen, denying them meals in the household. For he says that they are now of an age to earn their living and to trade at a profit as he did. He gives them some twenty or twenty-four groats apiece or the equivalent, to bargain with and make their profit. This he does so that they may gain experience and readiness in deals of all kinds and get accustomed to business. This is what the boys do. All day long they never stop running to and fro, buying this and that and then selling it. When the pearl fishery is in full swing, they hurry to the ports and buy five or six pearls from the fishers, according to the numbers they have to offer. Then they take them to the dealers, who stay indoors for fear of the sun, and say: 'Do you want these? I declare that they cost me so much. Allow me such profit as you think fit.' And the dealers give them something above the cost price. Then back they go; or else they say to the dealers: 'Would you like me to go and buy something?' In this way they become very clever and astute traders. They may take foodstuffs home for their mothers to cook and dress for them, but not so that they eat at their father's expense.

You must know that in this kingdom, and indeed throughout India, the beasts and birds are very different from ours – all except one bird, and that is the quail. The quails here are certainly like ours, but all the rest are very different. I assure you for a fact that there are bats here – that is, the birds that fly by night and have no feathers – which are as big as goshawks. There are goshawks as black as crows, a good deal bigger than ours and good fliers and hawkers. And let me add something else that is worth recounting: they feed their horses on flesh cooked with rice and many other cooked foods.

Let me tell you further that they have many idols in their monasteries, both male and female, and to these idols many maidens are offered in the following manner. Their mother and father offer them to certain idols, whichever they please. Once they have been offered, then whenever the monks of these idol monasteries require them to come to the monasteries to entertain the idol, they come as they are bidden; and sing and afford a lively entertainment. And there are great numbers of these maidens, because they form large bevies. Several times a week in every month they bring food to the idols to which they are dedicated; and I will explain how they bring it and how they say that the idol has eaten. Some of these maidens of whom I have spoken prepare tasty dishes of meat and other food and bring them to their idols in the monasteries. Then they lay the table before them, setting out the meal they have brought, and leave it for some time. Meanwhile they all sing and dance and afford the merriest sport in the world. And when they have disported themselves for as long a time as a great lord might spend in eating a meal, then they say that the spirit of the idols has eaten the substance of the food. Whereupon they take the food and eat together with great mirth and jollity. Finally they return – each to her own home. This they do until they take husbands. Such maidens are to be found in profusion throughout this kingdom, doing all the things of which I have told you. And the reason why they are called on to amuse the idols is this. The priests of the idols very often declare: 'The god is estranged from the goddess. One will not cohabit with the other, nor will they hold speech together. Since they are thus estranged and angry with each other, unless they are reconciled and make their peace, all our affairs will miscarry and go from bad to worse, because they will not bestow their blessing and their favour.' So these maidens go to the monastery as I have said. And there, completely naked, except that they cover their private parts, they sing before the god and goddess. The god stands by himself on an altar under a canopy, the goddess by herself on another altar under another canopy. And the people say that he often dallies with her, and they have intercourse together; but when they are estranged they refrain from intercourse, and then these maidens come to placate them. When they are there, they devote themselves to singing, dancing, leaping, tumbling, and every sort of exercise calculated to amuse the god and goddess and to reconcile them. And while they are thus entertaining them, they cry: 'O Lord, wherefore art thou wroth with thy Lady? Wherefore art thou grown cold towards her, and wherefore is thy spirit estranged? Is she not comely? Is she not pleasant? Assuredly, yea. May it please thee, therefore, to be reconciled with her and take thy delight with her; for assuredly she is exceedingly pleasant.' And then the maiden who has spoken these words will lift her leg higher than her neck and perform a pirouette for the delectation of the god and goddess. When they have had enough of this entertainment, they go home. In the morning the idol-priest will announce with great joy that he has seen the god consort with the goddess and that harmony is restored between them. And then everyone rejoices and gives thanks. The flesh of these maidens, so long as they remain maidens, is so hard that no one could grasp or pinch them in any place: for a penny they will allow a man to pinch them as hard as he can. After they are married their flesh remains hard, but not so hard as before. On account of this hardness, their breasts do not hang down, but remain upstanding and erect.

Men have their beds very lightly constructed of

canes, so designed that after they have got in, when they wish to sleep, they can hoist themselves with ropes up to the ceiling and make themselves fast there. This they do in order to avoid the tarantulas of which I have spoken, whose bite is noxious, besides fleas and other vermin; and also to catch the breeze and combat the heat. They do not all do this, but only the nobles and heads of houses. The others sleep on the highways. It is a proof of the excellent justice kept by the king that when a nocturnal traveller wishes to sleep and has with him a sack of pearls or other valuables – for men travel by night rather than by day, because it is cooler – he will put the sack under his head and sleep where he is; and no one ever loses anything by theft or otherwise. If he should lose it, he receives prompt satisfaction – so long, that is, as he has been sleeping on the highway; but not if he has been sleeping away from it. In that case the presumption is against him. For the authorities will inquire: 'Why were you sleeping away from the highway, if not because you had some dishonest intention?' Accordingly he is punished, and his loss will not be made good.

I have now told you a great deal about the manners and customs of this kingdom and the behaviour of its people. We will now leave it and go on to tell you of another kingdom, whose name is Motupalli.

Motupalli is a kingdom that is reached by travelling northwards from Maabar for about 1,000 miles. It is ruled by a queen, who is a very wise woman. For I assure you that it is fully forty years since the king her husband died. As she was deeply devoted to him, she said that God would not wish her to take another husband, since he whom she loved more than her own life was dead. That was why she declined to marry again. I can tell you that throughout her forty years' reign she has governed her kingdom well with a high standard of justice and equity, as her husband did before. And I assure you that never was lady or lord so well beloved as she is by her subjects.

The people here are idolaters and tributary to none. They live on rice, flesh, milk, fish, and fruit.

This kingdom produces diamonds. Let me tell you how they are got. You must know that in the kingdom there are many mountains in which the diamonds are found, as you will hear. When it rains the water rushes down through these mountains, scouring its way through mighty gorges and caverns. When the rain has stopped and the water has drained away, then men go in search of diamonds through these gorges from which the water has come, and they find plenty. In summer, when there is not a drop of water to be found, then diamonds can be found in plenty among these mountains. But the heat is so great that it is almost intolerable. Moreover the mountains are so infested with serpents of immense size and girth that men cannot go there without grave danger. But all the same they go there as best they can and find big stones of fine quality. Let me tell you further that these serpents are exceedingly venomous and noxious, so that men dare not venture into the caves where the serpents live. So they get the diamonds by other means. You must know that there is a big deep valley so walled in by precipitous cliffs that no one can enter it. But I will tell you what men do. They take many lumps of flesh imbrued in blood and fling them down into the depths of the valley. And the lumps thus flung down pick up great numbers of diamonds, which become embedded in the flesh. Now it so happens that these mountains are inhabited by a great many white eagles, which prey on the serpents. When these eagles spy the flesh lying at the bottom of the valley, down they swoop and seize the lumps and carry them off. The men observe attentively where the eagles go, and as soon as they see that a bird has alighted and is swallowing the flesh, they rush to the spot as fast as they can. Scared by their sudden approach, the eagles fly away, leaving the flesh behind. And when they get hold of it, they find diamonds in plenty embedded in it. Another means by which they get the diamonds is this. When the eagles eat the flesh, they also eat – that is, they swallow – the diamonds. Then at night, when the eagle comes back, it deposits the diamonds it has swallowed with its droppings. So men come and collect these droppings, and there too they find diamonds in plenty. Now you have heard three ways in which diamonds are gathered. And there are many others. You must know that in all the world diamonds are found nowhere else except in this kingdom alone. But there they are both abundant and of good quality. You must not suppose that diamonds of the first water come to our countries of Christendom. Actually they are exported to the Great Khan and to the kings and noblemen of these various regions and realms. For it is they who have the wealth to buy all the costliest stones.

Let us turn now to other matters. You should know that in this kingdom are made all the best buckrams in the world – those of the finest texture and the highest value. For I assure you that they resemble cloths of Rheims linen. There is no king or queen in the world who would not gladly wear a fabric of such delicacy and beauty. The country is well stocked with beasts, including the biggest sheep in the world, and with great abundance and variety of foodstuffs. As there is nothing else worth mentioning, we will leave this kingdom and tell you of the burial-place of Messer St Thomas the Apostle.

The body of St Thomas lies in the province of Maabar in a little town. There are few inhabitants, and merchants do not visit the place; for there is nothing in the way of merchandise that could be got from it, and it is a very out-of-the-way spot. But it is a great place of pilgrimage both for Christians and for Saracens. For I assure you that the Saracens of this country have great faith in him and declare that he was a Saracen and a great prophet and call him *avariun*, that is to say 'holy man.'

The Christians who guard the church have many palm-trees that yield wine and also such as bear coconuts. One of these nuts is a meal for a man, both meat and drink. Their outer husk is matted with fibres, which are employed in various ways and serve many useful purposes. Under this husk is a food that provides a square meal for a man. It is very tasty, as sweet as sugar and as white as milk, and is in the form of a cup like the surrounding husk. Inside this food is enough juice to fill a phial. The juice is clear and cool and admirably flavoured. When a man has eaten the kernel, he drinks the juice. And so from one nut a man can have his fill of meat and drink. For each of these trees the Christians pay one groat a month to one of the brothers who are kings in Maabar.

Let me tell you a marvellous thing about this burial-place. You must know that the Christians who go there on pilgrimage take some of the earth from the place where the saintly body died and carry it back to their own country. Then, when anyone falls sick of a quartan or tertian ague or some such fever, they give him a little of this earth to drink. And no sooner has he drunk than he is cured. The remedy never fails. And you should know that the earth is of a red colour.

Let me tell you further of a fine miracle that happened about the year of our Lord 1288. It so happened that a baron of this country had a great quantity of a certain grain called rice. And with this he filled all the houses round about the church. When the Christians who guard the church and the saintly body saw that this idolatrous lord was filling the houses in this way, so that pilgrims had nowhere to lodge, they took it very much to heart and begged him earnestly to desist. But he, being a ruthless and haughty man, paid no heed to their prayers, but continued to fill all the houses at his own pleasure without regard to the wishes of the Christians. It was then, when he had filled all the saint's houses and provoked the indignation of the brethren, that the great miracle happened, as I will tell you. On the night after he had filled them Messer St Thomas the Apostle appeared to him with a fork in his hand and held it to the baron's throat, saying: 'Either you will empty my houses forthwith, or if you do not you must needs die an evil death.' So saying, he pressed his throat hard, so that it seemed to the baron that he was in great pain and on the point of death. When he had done this, the saint departed. Next morning the baron arose early and ordered all the houses to be emptied. And he related all that the saint had done to him, which was accounted a great miracle. At this the Christians were filled with gladness and joy and rendered great thanks and great honour to Messer St Thomas and blessed his name exceedingly. And I assure you that many other miracles happen here all the year round, which would be reckoned great marvels by any who heard them, notably the curing of Christians whose bodies are disabled or crippled.

Now that we have told you of this, we should like to tell you how the saint met his death, as it is reported by the people of these parts. The truth is that Messer St Thomas was outside his hermitage in the wood, praying to the Lord his God. And round him were many peacocks – for you must know that they are more plentiful here than anywhere in the world. And while he was thus saying his prayers, an idolater of the race and lineage of the *gavi* let fly an arrow from his bow, intending to kill one of these peacocks who were round the saint. And he never saw the saint himself. But the shot intended for the peacock hit the saint on his right side. And when he had received the blow he worshipped his creator most fervently, and of that blow he died. But it is a fact that before he came to the place where he died he made many converts in Nubia – just how this happened we shall tell you in due order at the appropriate time and place.

To turn now to other matters, it is a fact that in this country when a child is born they anoint him once a week with oil of sesame, and this makes him grow much darker than when he was born. For I assure you that the darkest man is here the most highly esteemed and considered better than the others who are not so dark. Let me add that in very truth these people portray and depict their gods and their idols black and their devils white as snow. For they say that God and all the saints are black and the devils are all white. That is why they portray them as I have described. And similarly they make the images of their idols all black.

You must know that the men of this country have such a faith in the ox and such a high regard for its sanctity that when they are going to war they take some of the hair of the wild ox of which I have told you; and those who are horsemen set some of this ox-hair on their horse's mane, while foot-soldiers fasten it to their shields. Some also bind it into their own hair. This they do because they believe that by virtue of the ox-hair they will be more surely saved and rescued from all mishap. Such is the custom among all who go to war. For this reason the hair of the wild ox is highly prized here; for no one thinks himself safe without it. Let me tell you next of a province called Lar, which lies to westward of the place where St Thomas the Apostle is buried. From this province are sprung all the Brahmans in the world, and it is from here that they originate. I assure you that these Brahmans are among the best traders in the world and the most reliable. They would not tell a lie for anything in the world and do not utter a word that is not true. You must know that when a foreign trader comes to this province, knowing nothing of the manners and customs of the country, he will find one of these Brahman merchants and entrust his wealth and his wares to his keeping, requesting him to conduct his business on his behalf, lest he should be deceived through ignorance of local customs. Then the Brahman merchant will promptly take charge of the foreign merchant's wares and deal with them no less faithfully in buying and selling and look after the interests of the foreigner with no less care, indeed with more, than if they were his own. For this service he will ask no payment, unless the foreigner wishes to make him a present as an act of generosity. They eat no meat and drink no wine. They live very virtuous lives according to their own usage. They have no sexual intercourse except with their own wives. They take nothing that belongs to another. They would never kill a living creature or do any act that they believe to be sinful. And you must know that all the Brahmans in the world are known by an emblem which they wear. For they all carry a cord of cotton on their shoulder and fasten it across the chest, under the other arm, and back behind them. By this emblem they are known wherever they go. And I assure you that they have a rich king well endowed with treasures. This king is very anxious to buy pearls and other precious stones. So he has made a compact with all the merchants of his country that for all the pearls they bring from the kingdom of Maabar that they call Chola, which is the best province and the most refined in all India and the one in which the best pearls are found, he will pay them double the cost price. The Brahmans accordingly go to the kingdom of Maabar and buy all the good pearls they can get and take them to their king. They tell him truly how much they cost, and the king promptly pays them twice the amount. Thus they are never losers by the transaction. For this reason they have brought him a vast quantity of them of great size and excellent quality.

[. . .]

These Brahmans live longer than anyone else in the world. This is due to their light feeding and great abstinence. They have very good teeth, thanks to a herb they are accustomed to eat, which is a great aid to digestion and is very salutary to the human body. And you must know that these Brahmans do not practise phlebotomy or any other form of blood-letting.

Among them are certain men living under a rule who are called *Yogis*. They live even longer than the others, as much as 150 or 200 years. And their bodies remain so active that they can still come and go as they will and perform all the services required by their monastery and their idols and serve them just as well as if they were younger. This comes of their great abstinence and of eating very little food and only what is wholesome. For it is their practice to eat chiefly rice and milk. Let me tell you also of a special food they eat, which I am sure will strike you as remarkable. For I assure you that they take quicksilver and sulphur and mix them together and make a drink of them, which they then drink. They declare that this prolongs life, and so they live all the longer. They drink this mixture twice a month, and make a practice of it from childhood in order to live longer. And certainly those who live to such a great age are habituated to this drink of sulphur and quicksilver.

There is a regular religious order in this kingdom of Maabar, of those who are called by this name of *Yogi*, who carry abstinence to the extremes of which I will tell you and lead a harsh and austere life. You may take it for a fact that they go stark naked, wearing not a stitch of clothing nor even covering their private parts or any bodily member. They worship the ox, and most of them carry a little ox made of gilt copper or bronze in the middle of the forehead. You must understand that they wear it tied on. Let me tell you further that they burn cow-dung and make a powder of it. With this they anoint various parts of their body with great reverence, no less than Christians display in the use of holy water. If anyone does reverence to them while they are passing in the street, they anoint him with this powder on the forehead in token of blessing. They do not eat out of platters or on trenchers; but they take their food on the leaves of apples of paradise or other big leaves – not green leaves, but dried ones; for they say that the green leaves have souls, so that this would be a sin. For in their dealings with all living creatures they are at pains to do nothing that they believe to be a sin. Indeed they would sooner die than do anything that they deemed to be sinful. When other men ask them why they go naked and are not ashamed to show their sexual member, they say: 'We go naked because we want nothing of this world. For we came into the world naked and unclothed. The reason why we are not ashamed to show our member is that we commit no sin with it, so we are not more ashamed to show it than you are when you show your hand or face or any other member which you do not employ in sinful lechery. It is because you employ this member in sin and lechery that you cover it and are ashamed of it. But we are no more ashamed of it than of our fingers, because we commit no sin with it.' Such is the justification they offer to those who ask them why they are not ashamed of their nakedness. I assure you further that they would not kill any creature or any living thing in the world, neither fly nor flea nor louse nor any other vermin, because they say that they have souls. For the same reason they refuse to eat living things because of the sin they would incur. I assure you that they do not eat anything fresh, either herb or root, until it is dried; because they declare that while they are fresh they have souls. When they wish to relieve their bowels, they go to the beach or the sea-shore and there void their excrement in the sand by the water.

Then, after cleansing themselves in the water, they take a stick or rod, with which they spread out their excrement and so crumble it into the sand that nothing is visible. When asked why they do this, they reply: 'This would breed worms. And the worms thus created, when their food was consumed by the sun, would starve to death. And since that substance issues from our bodies – for without food we cannot live – we should incur grievous sin by the death of so many souls created of our substance. Therefore we annihilate this substance, so that no worms may be created from it merely to die of starvation by our guilt and default.' Let me tell you further that they sleep naked on the ground with nothing under them and nothing over them. It is truly marvellous that they do not die and that they live as long as I have told you. They also practice great abstinence in eating; for they fast all the year round and never drink anything but water.

Here is something else worth relating. They have their monks who live in monasteries to serve the idols. And this is the probation they must undergo before appointment to the office, when one has died and another is to be chosen in his place. The maidens who are offered to the idols are brought in and made to touch the probationers. They touch them on various parts of the body and embrace and fondle them and instil into them the uttermost of earthly bliss. If the man thus caressed lies completely motionless without any reaction to the maiden's touch, he passes muster and is admitted to their order. If on the other hand his member reacts to the touch, they will not keep him, but expel him forthwith, declaring that there is no place among them for a man of wantonness. So strict are these idolaters and so stubborn in their misbelief.

The reason they give for burning their dead is that if a body were not burnt it would breed worms; and when the worms had eaten it, they would inevitably die. And they say that by their death the souls of the deceased would incur great sin. That is their justification for cremating the dead. And they firmly maintain that worms have souls.

Now that we have told you of the customs of these idolaters, let us turn to a delightful story that I forgot to tell when we were dealing with Ceylon. You shall hear it for yourselves and I am sure it will impress you.

Ceylon, as I told you earlier in this book, is a large island. Now it is a fact that in this island there is a very high mountain, so ringed by sheer cliffs that no one can climb it except by one way, of which I will tell you. For many iron chains have been hung on the side of the mountain, so arranged that by their means a man can climb to the top. It is said that on the top of this mountain is the monument of Adam, our first parent. The Saracens say that it is Adam's grave, but the idolaters call it the monument of Sakyamuni Burkhan. This Sakyamuni was the first man in whose name idols were made. According to their traditions he was the best man who ever lived among them, and the first whom they revered as a saint and in whose name they made idols. He was the son of a rich and powerful king. He was a man of such virtuous life that he would

44

pay no heed to earthly things and did not wish to be king. When his father saw that he had no wish to be king or to care for any of the things of this world, he was deeply grieved. He made him a very generous offer: he promised to crown him king of the realm, so that he should rule it at his own pleasure – for he himself was willing to resign the crown and all his authority, so that his son should be sole ruler. His son replied that he would have none of it. When his father saw that he would not accept the kingship for anything in the world, his grief was so bitter that he came near to dying. And no wonder, because he had no other son and no one else to whom he might leave his kingdom. Then the king had recourse to the following scheme. For he resolved to find means of inducing his son to give his mind willingly to earthly things and accept the crown and the kingdom. So he housed him in a very luxurious palace and provided 30,000 maidens of the utmost beauty and charm to minister to him. For no male was admitted, but only these maidens; maidens waited on him at bed and board and kept him company all day long. They sang and danced before him and did all they could to delight him as the king had bidden them. But I assure you that all these maidens could not tempt the king's son to any wantonness, but he lived more strictly and more chastely than before. So he continued to lead a life of great virtue according to their usage. He was such a delicately nurtured youth that he had never been out of the palace and had never seen a dead man nor one who was not in full bodily health. For the king let no old or disabled man enter his presence. Now it happened that this youth was out riding one day along the road when he saw a dead man. He paused aghast, as one who had never seen the like, and immediately asked those who were with him what this was. They told him that it was a dead man. 'How, then?' cried the king's son. 'Do all men die?' 'Yes, truly,' said they. Then the youth said nothing but rode on his way deep in thought. He had not ridden far when he found a very old man who could not walk and had not a tooth in his head but had lost them all through old age. When the king's son saw this greybeard, he asked what was this and why could he not walk. And his companions told him that it was through old age that he had lost the power to walk and his teeth. When the king's son had learnt the truth about the dead man and the old one, he returned to his palace and resolved that he would stay no longer in this evil world, but would set out in search of him who never dies and who has created him. So he left the palace and his father and took his way into the high and desolate mountains; and there he spent the rest of his days most virtuously and chastely and in great austerity. For assuredly, had he been a Christian, he would have been a great saint with our Lord Jesus Christ.

When this prince died, he was brought to the king his father. And when the king saw that the son whom he loved more than himself was dead, there is no need to ask if he was stricken with grief and bitterness. First he ordered a solemn mourning. Then he had an image made in his likeness, all of gold and precious stones, and caused it to be honoured by all the people of the country and worshipped as a god. And they said that he had died eighty-four times. For they say that when he died the first time he became an ox; then he died a second time and became a horse. And in this manner they say that he died eighty-four times, and that every time he became an animal – a dog or some other creature. But the eighty-fourth time he died and became a god. And he is deemed by the idolaters to be the best and greatest god they have. And you must know that this was the first idol ever made by the idolaters and hence come all the idols in the world. And this happened in the island of Ceylon in India.

Now you have heard how idols first originated. Let me tell you next that idolaters from very distant parts come here on pilgrimage, just as Christians go to the shrine of Messer St James. And the idolaters say that the monument on this mountain is that of the king's son of whom you have just heard, and that the teeth and the hair and the bowl that are here also belonged to this prince, whose name was Sakyamuni Burkhan, that is to say, Sakyamuni the Saint. And the Saracens, who also come here in great numbers on pilgrimage, say that it is the monument of Adam our first parent and that the teeth and hair and bowl were his also. So now you have heard how the idolaters say that he is that king's son who was their first idol and their first god, while the Saracens say that he is Adam our first parent. But God alone knows who he is or what he was. For we do not believe that Adam is in this place, since our Scripture of Holy Church declares that he is in another part of the world.

Now it happened that the Great Khan heard that on this mountain was the monument of Adam and likewise his teeth and his hair and the bowl from which he used to eat. He made up his mind that he must have these relics. So he sent here a great embassy in the year of our Lord 1284. What more shall I say? You may take it for a fact that the Great Khan's envoys with a great retinue set out on their way and journeyed so far by sea and land that they came to the island of Ceylon. They went to the king and so far succeeded in their mission that they acquired the two maxillary teeth, which were very large and thick, and some of the hair and the bowl, which was made of a very lovely green porphyry. With these acquisitions, they went their way and returned to their lord. And when they approached the great city of Khan-balik where the Great Khan was, they sent him word that they were coming and were bringing what they had been sent to fetch. Then the Great Khan ordered that all the people, both monks and others, should go out to meet these relics, which they were given to understand belonged to Adam. Why make a long story of it? Suffice it that all the people of Khan-balik went out to meet these relics and the monks received them and brought them to the Great Khan, who welcomed them with great joy and great ceremony and great reverence. And I assure you that they found in their scriptures a passage declaring that the bowl possessed this property that if anyone set in it food for one man he would have enough for five. And the Great Khan announced that he had had this put to the proof and that it was quite true.

That is how the Great Khan came by these relics of which you have heard; and what they cost him in treasure amounted to no small sum.

Now that we have told you the truth of the story in due order, let us turn to other matters.

First of all, let me tell you of the great and splendid city of Kayal. It belongs to Ashar, the eldest of the royal brothers. And you may take it that this is the port of call for all ships trading with the west – that is with Hormuz and Kais and Aden and all Arabia – for horses and other goods. The merchants use it as a port because it is conveniently situated and affords a good market for their wares. And merchants congregate here from many parts to buy horses and various merchandise. This king is very rich in treasure; he decks his person with many gems of great price and goes about in right royal state. He governs his country well and maintains strict justice, especially in his dealings with merchants who resort thither – that is, the foreign merchants. He maintains their interests with great rectitude. So merchants are very glad to come here because of this good king who safeguards them so well. And it is a fact that they make great profits here and their trade prospers.

Further, I would have you know that this king has fully 300 wives and more; for here a man is more highly esteemed in proportion as he supports more wives. When a quarrel breaks out between these five kings, who are brothers german, sprung from one father and one mother, and they have a mind to fight with one another, then their mother, who is still alive, intervenes between them and will not let them fight. Often it happens, when her sons will not be restrained by her prayers but persist in their determination to fight, that their mother seizes a knife and cries: 'If you do not stop quarrelling and make peace together, I will kill myself here and now. And first I will cut off the breasts from my bosom with which I gave you milk.' When the sons see how deeply their mother is grieved and how tenderly she pleads with them, and reflect that it is for their own good, then they come to terms and make peace. This has happened several times. But I assure you that after their mother's death a violent quarrel will infallibly break out amongst them and they will destroy one another.

You should know that these people, and indeed all the peoples of India, are addicted to the habit, which affords them some satisfaction, of carrying almost continually in their mouths a certain leaf called *tambur*. They go about chewing this leaf and spitting out the resulting spittle. This habit prevails especially among the nobles and magnates and kings. They mix the leaves with camphor and other spices and also with lime, and go about continually chewing them. And this habit is very beneficial to their health. If anyone is offended with somebody and wishes to insult and affront him, then when he meets him in the street he collects this mixture in his mouth and spits it in the other's face, saying: 'You are not worth this,' that is to say, what he has spat out. The other, regarding this as a deadly insult and outrage, promptly complains to the king that he has been slighted and dishonoured and craves leave to avenge himself. If the insult was directed against him and his clan, he will beg leave to match his person and his clan against the challenger's person and clan and prove whether or not he is worth no more than this; if it is a purely personal affront, then he will beg leave to settle it man to man. Then the king grants leave to both parties. If the contest is between clan and clan, each leader prepares for battle with his own following; and the only cuirass they don and wear for their protection is the skin their mother gave them at birth. When they are on the field, they strike, wound, and slay; for their swords strike home easily and a ready entry lies open to each of them. The king will be present in person and a multitude of spectators to watch the proceedings. When the king sees that many have been slain on either side and that one party appear to be gaining the upper hand and downing their adversaries, he will put between his teeth one end of a cloth that he has wrapped round him and hold out the other end at arm's length. Then the combatants cease forthwith from combat, and not another blow is struck. This is a frequent outcome. If the combat is between man and man, it will go like this. Both duellists will be naked, as they normally are, and each will have a knife. They are adept at defending themselves with these knives; for with these they parry a blow as nimbly as they inflict one. This, then, is the procedure. As you have learnt, they are dark-skinned people. So one of them will draw a circle in white on the other's flesh, wherever he may choose, and say to him: 'Know that

I will strike you within that circle and nowhere else. Guard yourself as best you can.' And the other will do as much to him. Then well for the better man, and for the worse, worse! For assuredly the blow that is first to reach its target does not go unfelt.

Now that we have said so much about this king, let us go on to speak of the realm of Quilon, which lies about 500 miles south-west of Maabar. The people are idolaters, though there are some Christians and Jews among them. They speak a language of their own. The king is tributary to none. Now I will tell you what is found in this kingdom and what are its products.

You must know that this country produces Quilon brazil which is very good, and also pepper in great abundance in all the fields and woods. Pepper is gathered in the months of May, June, and July. And I can tell you that the pepper trees are planted and watered and grow in cultivation. There is also plenty of good indigo, which is produced from a herb: they take this herb without the roots and put it in a big tub and add water and leave it till the herb is all rotted. Then they leave it in the sun, which is very hot and makes it evaporate and coagulate into a paste. Then it is chopped up into small pieces, as you have seen it. The heat here is so intense and the sun so powerful that it is scarcely tolerable. For I assure you that if you put an egg into one of the rivers you would not have long to wait before it boiled. Let me inform you further that merchants come here from Manzi and Arabia and the

Levant and ply a thriving trade; for they bring various products from their own countries by sea and export others in return.

The country produces a diversity of beasts different from those of all the rest of the world. There are black lions with no other visible colour or mark. There are parrots of many kinds. Some are entirely white – as white as snow – with feet and beaks of scarlet. Others are scarlet and blue – there is no lovelier sight than these in the world. And there are some very tiny ones, which are also objects of great beauty. Then there are peacocks of another sort than ours and much bigger and handsomer, and hens too that are unlike ours. What more need I say? Everything there is different from what it is with us and excels both in size and beauty. They have no fruit the same as ours, no beast, no bird. This is a consequence of the extreme heat. They have no grain excepting only rice. They make wine out of sugar, and a very good drink it is, and makes a man drunk sooner than grape wine. All that the human body needs for its living is to be had in profusion and very cheap with the one exception of grain other than rice. They have no lack of skilled astrologers. They have physicians who are adept at preserving the human body in health. They are all black-skinned and go stark naked, both males and females except for gay loin-cloths. They regard no form of lechery or sensual indulgence as sin. Their marriage customs are such that a man may wed his cousin german or his father's widow or his brother's. And these customs prevail throughout the Indies. Now that I have told you something of this kingdom – all that is worth recounting – let us move on to Comorin.

Comorin is a country of India proper in which it first becomes possible to see the Pole Star, which we have not seen all the way here since we left Java. From this place you can go out thirty miles into the sea and catch a glimpse of the Pole Star rising out of the water for about one cubit. This is not a highly civilized place, but decidedly savage. There are beasts of various sorts, notably monkeys, some of them of such distinctive appearance that you might take them for men. There are also the apes called 'Paul cats', so peculiar that they are a real marvel. Lions, leopards, and lynxes abound. As there is nothing else worth noting, we will pass on to Ely.

Ely is a kingdom about 300 miles west of Comorin. The people are idolaters, ruled by their own king, paying tribute to none and speaking a language of their own. I will tell you plainly of the customs and products of this country; and you will be able to understand them better, because we are now approaching more civilized places. In this province or kingdom there is no port, except that there is a big river with a very fine estuary. Pepper grows here in great abundance, and ginger too, besides plenty of other spices. The king is very rich in treasure, but not strong in man-power. However, the entrance to his kingdom is so easily defensible that no hostile army could force an entry; so he has no fear of anyone.

Let me tell you something else. Should it happen that a ship enters the estuary and goes upstream, if it is not a ship that is bound for this place they seize it and appropriate the whole cargo. They say: 'You were bound elsewhere and God has sent you to me, so that I may take all you have.' Thereupon they seize all the goods in the ship and keep them for their own and do not consider that they have done anything wrong. This practice prevails throughout all these provinces of India. If any ship is driven by stress of weather to put in at any place other than its proper destination, it is seized the moment it comes ashore and robbed of everything on board. For the inhabitants will say: 'You meant to go somewhere else; but my good luck and merit have brought you here, so that I should have all your possessions.'

You should know that ships from Manzi and elsewhere come here in summer, load in four to eight days, and leave as soon as they can, because there is no port and it is very hazardous to linger here, because there are merely sandy beaches without any port. It is true, however, that ships of Manzi are not so much afraid to beach on sand as others are, because they are fitted with such powerful wooden anchors that they hold firm in every stress.

There are lions here and other beasts of prey, besides game in plenty.

We shall tell you next of the great kingdom of Malabar, which lies further west and has a king and a language of its own. The people here are idolaters, tributary to

55

none. Here the Pole Star is more clearly visible, seeming to rise about two cubits above the water. You must know that from Malabar, and from a neighbouring province called Gujarat, more than 100 ships cruise out every year as corsairs, seizing other ships and robbing the merchants. For they are pirates on a big scale. I assure you that they bring their wives and little children with them. They spend the whole summer on a cruise and work havoc among the merchants. Most of these villainous corsairs scatter here and there, scouring the sea in quest of merchant ships. But sometimes their evil-doing is more concerted. For they cruise in line, that is to say at distances of about five miles apart. In this way twenty ships cover 100 miles of sea. And as soon as they catch sight of a merchant ship, one signals to another by means of beacons, so that not a ship can pass through this sea undetected. But the merchants, who are quite familiar with the habits of these villainous corsairs and know that they are sure to encounter them, go so well armed and equipped that they are not afraid to face them after they have been detected. They defend themselves stoutly and inflict great damage on their attackers. But of course it is inevitable that one should be captured now and then. When the corsairs do capture a merchant ship, they help themselves to the ship and the cargo; but they do not hurt the men. They say to them: 'Go and fetch another cargo. Then, with luck, you may give us some more.'

In this kingdom there is great abundance of pepper and also of ginger, besides cinnamon in plenty and other spices, turbit and coconuts. Buckrams are made here of the loveliest and most delicate texture in the world. Many other articles of merchandise are exported. In return, when merchants come here from overseas they load their ships with brass, which they use as ballast, cloth of gold and silk, sendal, gold, silver, cloves, spikenard, and other such spices that are not produced here. You must know that ships come here from very many parts, notably from the great province of Manzi, and goods are exported to many parts. Those that go to Aden are carried thence to Alexandria.

Now that we have told you of Malabar, we shall go on to speak of Gujarat. You must understand that we do not enumerate all the cities of these kingdoms, since the list would be far too long. For every kingdom has cities and towns in plenty.

Gujarat likewise is a great kingdom. The people are idolaters and have a king and a language of their own and pay tribute to none. The country lies towards the west. Here the Pole Star is still more clearly visible, with an apparent altitude of six cubits. In this kingdom are the most arrant corsairs in the world. Let me tell you one of their nasty tricks. You must know that, when they capture merchants, they make them drink tamarind and sea-water, so that they pass or vomit up all the contents of their stomachs. Then the corsairs collect all that they have cast up and rummage through it to see if it contains any pearls or precious stones. For the corsairs say that when the merchants are captured they swallow their pearls and other gems to prevent their discovery. That is why they do not scruple to treat them to this drink.

There is pepper here in profusion and also ginger and indigo. There is also plenty of cotton, for the cotton trees grow here to a great height – as much as six paces after twenty years' growth. But when they reach this age they no longer produce cotton fit for spinning, but only for use in wadding or padded quilts. The growth of these trees is such that up to twelve years they produce cotton for spinning, but from twelve to twenty an inferior fibre only.

The manufactures of this kingdom include great quantities of leather goods, that is, the tanned hides of goat and buffalo, wild ox and unicorn and many other beasts. Enough is manufactured to load several ships a year. They are exported to Arabia and many other countries. For this kingdom supplies many other kingdoms and provinces. They also manufacture handsome mats of scarlet leather, embossed with birds and beasts and stitched with gold and silver of very fine workmanship. They are so exquisite that they are a marvel to behold. You must understand that these leather mats of which I speak are such as the Saracens sleep on, and very good they are for the purpose. They also make cushions stitched with gold, so splendid that they are worth fully six marks of silver. And some of the mats are of such a quality that they are worth ten marks of silver. What more need I say? Suffice it that in this kingdom are produced leather goods of more consummate workmanship than anywhere in the world and of higher value.

Now that we have told you the facts about this

kingdom in due order, we shall go on our way and tell you next of a kingdom called Thana.

Thana is a large and splendid kingdom lying towards the west. It is ruled by a king and tributary to none. The people are idolaters and speak a language of their own. Pepper is not produced there in quantities, nor any other spice, as in the other kingdoms of which we have been speaking. There is no lack of incense, but it is not white but tinged with brown. This is a busy centre of commerce and a great resort of merchant shipping, exporting leather goods worked in various styles of excellent quality and design. It also exports plenty of good buckram and cotton as well. And merchants import in their ships gold and silver and brass and many other goods which the kingdom requires in exchange for such wares as they hope to sell profitably elsewhere.

Here is another item which is not creditable. I must tell you that this kingdom is the base for many corsairs who sally out to sea and take a heavy toll of merchant shipping. And, what is more, they act with the connivance of the king. For he has struck a bargain with the corsairs that they shall give him all the horses they may capture. And these form a considerable part of their booty, because, as I have mentioned earlier, there is a lively export trade in horses to all parts of India and few ships go thither without taking horses. That is why the king has made this bargain with the corsairs, by which they give him all the horses they take, while all the rest of the merchandise – gold, silver, and precious stones – they keep for themselves. Now this is a shameful compact and unworthy of a king.

Let us now pass on and talk of Cambay, a great kingdom lying towards the west. It has a king and a language of its own and is tributary to none. The people are idolaters. From this kingdom the Pole Star is seen more clearly; for the further you go towards the west, the better view you get of the Pole Star. This kingdom is the centre of an active commerce. Indigo is plentiful here and of good quality. Buckram and cotton are produced in abundance for export to many provinces and kingdoms. There is also a brisk trade in leather goods of various style and manufacture, and this is on a big scale because the standards of workmanship is as high here as anywhere. There is also a wide range of other goods of which I will make no mention, as it would be tedious to enumerate them. Many merchant ships call here with various imports, especially gold, silver, and brass. They bring in the products of their own countries and take out such local products as they hope to sell at a profit. You must know that in this kingdom there are no corsairs; the people live by trade and industry and are honest folk. There is nothing else worth mentioning.

Leaving Cambay, we come to the great kingdom of Somnath, which lies towards the west. The people are idolaters with a king and language of their own and tributary to none. They are not corsairs but live by trade and industry, as honest folk ought to do. For you may take it for a fact that this is a kingdom in which commerce thrives, a resort of merchants from many lands bringing in their wares and exporting others in return. Yet I must add that the people are harsh and stubborn in their idolatry. As there is nothing else worthy of note, we shall go on to speak of Kech-Makran.

This is a great kingdom with a king and language of its own. Some of the people are idolaters, but most are Saracens. They live by trade and industry. They have rice and wheat in profusion. The staple foods are rice, meat, and milk. Merchants come here in great numbers by sea and by land with a variety of merchandise and export the products of the kingdom. There is nothing else worthy of note.

I must tell you that this kingdom is the last province of India, in the quarter between west and north-west. All that lies between Maabar and this province – that is, all the kingdoms and provinces I have described from Maabar to here – constitute Greater India, the best part of all the Indies. You must know that of this Greater India I have described only those provinces and cities that lie on the sea-coast. Of the inland regions I have told you nothing; for the tale would be too long in the telling. So we shall now leave this province and I will tell you of certain islands which also form part of the Indies.

Madagascar, Zanzibar and the Islands and Kingdoms of the Arabian Sea

Let us begin with two islands called Male Island and Female Island. Male Island lies in the sea some 500 miles south of Kech-Makran. The inhabitants are baptized Christians, observing the rule and customs of the Old Testament. For when a man's wife is pregnant he does not touch her again till she has given birth. After this he continues to abstain for another forty days. Then he touches her again as he will. But I assure you that in this island the men do not live with their wives or with any other women; but all the women live on the other island, which is called Female Island. You must know that the men of Male Island go over to Female Island and stay there for three months, that is March, April, and May. For these three months the men stay in the other island with their wives and take their pleasure with them. After this they return to their own island and get on with their business. I must tell you that in Male Island is found ambergris of fine quality. The inhabitants live on rice, milk, and meat. They are very good fishermen and catch so many good fish that they dry great quantities of them, so that they have plenty to eat all the year round and also sell them to others. They have no lord except a bishop, who in turn is subject to the archbishop of Socotra. They speak a language of their own. Male Island is about thirty miles distant from Female Island. According to their own account, their reason for not staying all the year round with their wives is that if they did so they could not live. The sons who are born are nursed by their mothers in Female Island till they are fourteen years old, when they are sent to join their fathers in Male Island. When the men come to Female Island they sow the corn, which the women till and reap. The women also gather fruits, which grow there in great profusion. Otherwise they have nothing to do except to rear the children. Such then are the customs of these two islands. As there is nothing else worth mentioning, we shall go on to tell of Socotra.

The island of Socotra lies about 500 miles south of these two. The inhabitants are baptized Christians and have an archbishop. Ambergris is found here in great quantities. It is produced in the belly of the whale and the cachalot, which are the two biggest fish that exist in the sea. We shall tell you how whales are caught in these parts. The whale fishers have a lot of tunny fish, which they catch only for this purpose. These fish, which are very fat, they chop up small and put in big jars or pots, to which they add salt, making a plentiful supply of pickle. This done, a dozen or so of the fishers will take a small ship and loading her with these fish, and with all the pickle or briny fish-broth, will put out to sea. Then they will take certain remnants of rags or other refuse and tying them together in a bundle dip

them in the pickle, which is very greasy. Having cast
the bundle into the sea attached by a line to the ship,
they will hoist sail and spend that day cruising to and
fro on the high sea. Wherever they go, the grease in
the pickle leaves a sort of trail over the water, recogniz-
able by its oiliness. If it happens to pass by a place
where a whale is, or the whale catches wind of the
tunny fat lingering in the wake of the ship, he follows
the trail by the scent of the tunny even for a hundred
miles, if the vessel has sailed so far – so greedy is he to
get at the tunny. When he has come so near the vessel
that those on board catch sight of him, they throw him
two or three morsels of tunny. When he has eaten he
becomes intoxicated, as a man is with wine. Then some
of them climb on his back, carrying an iron harpoon
so barbed that once driven in it cannot be pulled out.
One of them will stand this harpoon on the whale's
head, while another hits it with a wooden mallet and
immediately drives it home to its full length. For the
whale in his drunken stupor scarcely feels the men on
his back, so that they can do what they like. To the
butt end of the harpoon is fastened a stout rope fully
300 paces long. At every fifty paces along the rope is
fastened a cask and a plank. To the top of the cask is
attached a flag, and at the bottom end is a counterpoise,
so that the cask does not roll over but the flag stands
upright. The last lap of the rope is made fast to a boat
which they have with them. This boat will be manned
by a few of the whalers, so that when the whale feeling
himself wounded turns to flight, those who climbed
on him to drive in the harpoon and are now left in the

water may swim to the boat and scramble aboard. Then one of the casks is thrown into the water with the flag, thus allowing fifty paces of rope. When the whale dives and makes off, the boat to which the rope is fastened is towed along after him. If the whale seems to be pulling downwards too strongly, another cask with another flag is thrown overboard. And so, as he cannot pull down the casks under water, he becomes exhausted with towing them and finally succumbs to his wound and dies. The ship follows after, guided by the sight of the flags. When the whale is dead, the ship takes him in tow. Afterwards they bring him ashore on their island or a neighbouring one, where they sell him. And on a single whale they may clear a net profit of 1,000 *livres*. This, then, is how they catch them.

The islanders produce fine cotton cloths and other merchandise in plenty, notably great quantities of salt fish – big fish of excellent quality. They live on rice, meat, and milk; for they have no other grain. They go stark naked, after the fashion of the other Indians who are idolaters. Many merchant ships visit this island with all sorts of goods for sale and export the local products at a good profit. You must know that all the merchant ships bound for Aden call in at this island.

I should explain that the archbishop of Socotra has nothing to do with the Pope at Rome, but is subject to an archbishop who lives at Baghdad. The archbishop of Baghdad sends out the archbishop of this island; and he also sends out many others to different parts of the world, just as the Pope does. And these clergy and prelates owe obedience not to the church of Rome but to this great prelate of Baghdad whom they have as their Pope. Let me tell you further that many corsairs put in at this island at the end of a cruise and pitch camp here and sell their booty. And I assure you that they find a ready market, because the Christians of the island know that all these goods have been stolen from idolaters and Saracens, not from Christians, so they have no compunction in buying them. You should know also that, if the archbishop of Socotra dies, his successor must be sent from Baghdad; otherwise there could never be an archbishop here.

I give you my word that the Christians of this island are the most expert enchanters in the world. It is true that the archbishop does not approve of these enchantments and castigates and rebukes them for the practice. But this has no effect, because they say that their forefathers did these things of old and they are resolved to go on doing them. And the archbishop cannot override their resolve; but what he cannot cure he must needs endure. So the Christians of the island go on with their enchantments at their own sweet will. Let me tell you something about them. You may take it for a fact that these enchanters perform feats of many kinds and in no small measure bring about what they desire. If a pirate ship has done some damage to the islanders, she cannot sail from the island without first making amends for the damage done. She may set sail before a favouring breeze and make some headway on her course; but they will conjure up a headwind and force her to turn back. They can make the wind blow from whatever quarter they may wish. They can calm the sea at will, or raise a raging storm and a howling gale. They are masters of many other marvellous enchantments; but I think it better not to speak of these in this book, because these enchantments produce effects which, were men to hear of them, might set them marvelling overmuch. So let us leave it at that and say no more.

As there is nothing else worth mentioning in the island, we shall pass on to Madagascar. Madagascar is an island lying about 1,000 miles south of Socotra. The people are Saracens who worship Mahomet. They have four *sheikhs* – that is to say, four elders – who exercise authority over the whole island. You must know that this island is one of the biggest and best in the whole world. It is said to measure about 4,000 miles in circumference. The people live by trade and industry. More elephants are bred here than in any other province; and I assure you that not so many elephant tusks are sold in all the rest of the world put together as in this island and that of Zanzibar. The meat eaten here is only camel-flesh. The number of camels slaughtered every day is so great that no one who had not seen it for himself could credit the report of it. They say that camel-flesh is better and more wholesome than any other; that is why they eat it all the year round. The island produces scarlet sandal-wood trees as big as the trees of our country. These trees would fetch a high price anywhere else; but here they have whole woods of them, as we have of other wild trees. They have plenty of ambergris, because whales abound in these seas, and also cachalots. And since they catch great numbers of both, they are never short of ambergris; for you know it is the whale that produces ambergris. They have leopards and lynxes and lions also in great numbers. Other beasts, such as harts, stags, and roe-buck and such-like game animals, are also abundant, besides game-birds of many kinds. There are also many ostriches of huge size. The great diversity of birds, quite different from ours, is truly marvellous. Many marketable commodities are produced here. And many ships come here laden with cloth of gold and various silken fabrics, and much else besides that I will not attempt to specify, and exchange them for local products. They arrive and depart with full cargoes and the merchants make a handsome profit on the transaction.

I should add that ships cannot sail to the other islands that lie farther south, beyond Madagascar and Zanzibar, because the current sets so strongly towards the south that they would have little chance of returning. Therefore they do not venture to go. You may note that ships coming from Maabar to this island make the voyage in twenty days, whereas the return trip takes them all of three months; and this is due to the continual southward set of the current. It flows in the same direction all the time – southward, ever southward. These more southerly islands, which men do not willingly visit because of this southward drift, are very numerous, and it is said that they are inhabited by gryphon birds, which make their appearance here at certain seasons of the year. But you must know that they are by no means such as men in our country suppose, or as we portray them – half bird and half lion. According to the report of those who have seen them, it is not true that they are a blend of bird and lion; but I assure you that these men, the actual eye-witnesses, report that in build they are just like eagles but of the most colossal size. Let me tell you first what these eye-witnesses report and then what I have seen myself. They report that they are so huge and bulky that one of them can pounce on an elephant and carry it up to a great height in the air. Then it lets go, so that the elephant drops to earth and is smashed to pulp, whereupon the gryphon bird perches on the carcass and feeds at its ease. They add that they have a wing-span of thirty paces and their wing-feathers are twelve paces long and of a thickness proportionate to their length. What I have seen myself I will tell you elsewhere, since that fits in better with the plan of the book.

Now that I have given you this second-hand account of the gryphon bird, let me add that the Great Khan sent special emissaries here to learn about these islands, and again to treat for the release of a previous emissary who had been detained as a captive. And these later emissaries, and the other who had been held captive, had much to tell him of the marvels of these strange islands. I assure you that they brought back with them the tusks of a wild boar of monstrous size. He had one of them weighed and found that its weight was 14 lb. You may infer for yourselves what must have been the size of the boar that had such tusks as this. Indeed they declare that some of these boars are as big as buffaloes. There are also giraffes in plenty, and wild asses too.

Altogether their beasts and birds are so different from ours that it is a marvel to hear tell of them and a greater marvel to behold them. To return for a moment to the gryphon birds, I should explain that the islanders call them *rukhs* and know them by no other name and have no idea what a gryphon is. But I feel sure from the monstrous size they attribute to the birds that they cannot be anything but gryphons.

Now that we have told you everything worth mentioning about this island and its specialities, we shall go on to tell of Zanzibar.

Zanzibar is a large and splendid island some 2,000 miles in circumference. The people are all idolaters. They have a king and a language of their own and pay tribute to none. They are a big-built race, and though their height is not proportionate to their girth they are so stout and so large-limbed that they have the appearance of giants. I can assure you that they are also abnormally strong, for one of them can carry a load big enough for four normal men. And no wonder, when I tell you that they eat food enough for five. They are quite black and go entirely naked except that they cover their private parts. Their hair is so curly that it can scarcely be straightened out with the aid of water. They have big mouths and their noses are so flattened and their lips and eyes so big that they are horrible to look at. Anyone who saw them in another country would say that they were devils.

They have elephants in plenty and drive a brisk trade in their tusks. They also have lions of a different sort

from those found elsewhere, besides lynxes and leopards. What need of more words? They have all their
animals different from those of the rest of the world. I
can assure you that all their sheep are of one sort and
one colour, that is, they are all white with black heads;
in all the island you will not find ram or ewe that is
not of this pattern. There are also many giraffes, which
are very beautiful creatures to look at. Let me describe
their appearance. You must know that the giraffe is
short in the body and slopes down towards the rear,
because its hind legs are short; but the front legs and
neck are so long that the head is fully three paces above
the ground. It has a small head and does no harm to
anyone. Its colour is dappled red and white. And a very
pretty sight it is. About elephants, let me add one fact
that I forgot to mention: when the male wishes to
cover the female, he makes a hollow in the ground and
lays her in a supine position and mounts her in human
fashion, because her genital organs are situated very
near to the belly.

The women of this island are very ugly to look at.
They have huge mouths, huge eyes, and huge noses,
and their breasts are four times as big as those of other
women. Altogether, their appearance is quite repulsive.

The staple diet here is rice, meat, milk, and dates.
They have no grape wine; but they make a wine of rice
and sugar and spices, and a very good drink it is. A
brisk trade is plied here; for many merchant ships call
at the island with a great variety of goods, all of which
they dispose of before taking in a return cargo – chiefly
of elephant tusks, which are very abundant here. There

is also no lack of ambergris, since whales are caught in great numbers.

You should know that the men of the island are good fighters and acquit themselves very manfully in battle; for they are very brave and almost without fear of death. They have no horses, but fight on camels and elephants. They erect castles on the elephants' backs and cover them well and then climb up – from sixteen to twenty men together – armed with lances, swords, and stones. And this fighting on elephant-back is a formidable business. They have no arms but leather shields, lances, and swords, and the slaughter on both sides is heavy. Here is another point: when they are about to drive their elephants into the fray, they let them drink freely of their wine – that is, their own drink. This they do because, when an elephant has drunk his wine, he grows more ferocious and mettlesome and acquits himself proportionately better in battle.

Now we have told you a great part of what there is to tell about this island, its people, its fauna, and its products. As there is nothing else worth mentioning, we shall go on to speak of the great province of Abyssinia. But first we shall tell you one more thing about the Indies. You may take it for a fact that we have spoken only of the most distinguished provinces and kingdoms and islands, because there is no man in all the world who could tell the truth about all the islands of the Indies. But I have told you of the best and the flower of them all. For you must understand that a considerable portion of the other islands of which I have made no mention are subject to those I have described. And you may know that in the Indian Ocean there are 12,700 islands, inhabited and uninhabited, as shown by the maps and writings of the practised seamen who ply in these waters. Now we have done with Greater India, which extends from Maabar to Kech-Makran and comprises thirteen major kingdoms of which we have described ten. Lesser India runs from Chamba to Motupalli and comprises eight major kingdoms. And be it always understood that I am here speaking only of kingdoms on the mainland and not counting the islands, which make up a vast number of kingdoms.

And now let us turn to the great province Abyssinia, which is Middle India. You must know that the chief king of all this province is a Christian. And the other kings of the province, who are subject to him, number six, of whom three are Christians and three Saracens. The Christians of this province are distinguished by three marks on their faces, one from the forehead to the middle of the nose and one on either cheek. These marks are made by branding with a hot iron. And this is their baptism; for after they have been baptized in water, they are branded with this sign, which is a token of rank and a completion of the baptism. This is done when they are small; and they regard the custom not only as a badge of dignity but as an aid to health. There are also Jews in this country; and they have two marks, one on either cheek. And the Saracens have one mark only, that is, from the forehead to the middle of the nose. The Great King lives in the centre of the province, the Saracens over in the direction of Aden. In this province Messer St Thomas the Apostle preached. And after making some converts here he went to Maabar, where he met his death and where his body lies, as we have told you earlier in the book. And you must know that this great province of Abyssinia has many doughty men at arms and accomplished horsemen and no lack of horses. And there is great need of them. For they are at war with the Sultan of Aden and the Nubians and many others. Let me tell you a notable episode that took place in the year of our Lord 1288.

The truth is that this sovereign lord of the province of Abyssinia, who is a Christian, expressed his wish to go on pilgrimage to worship at the sepulchre of Christ in Jerusalem. The barons declared that it would be too hazardous for him to go in person and recommended him instead to send a bishop or some other great prelate. The king acceded to their recommendation. He sent for a bishop who was a man of very saintly life and told him that he wished him to go in his place as far as Jerusalem to worship at the sepulchre of our Lord Jesus Christ. The bishop promised to do his bidding, as that of his liege lord. The king bade him make ready and set out with all possible speed.

What more shall I say? The bishop took leave of the king and made ready and started on his way in the guise of a pilgrim, very honourably arrayed. He journeyed so far by sea and land that he came to Jerusalem. He went straight to the sepulchre and worshipped there and did to it such reverence and honour as a Christian ought to do to such a holy and venerable thing as is this sepulchre. And he made a great offering there on behalf of the king who had sent him. When the bishop had done all that he came to do well and wisely, like the wise man that he was, then he set out on the homeward journey with all his company. He continued on his way till he came to Aden. Now you must know that in this country Christians are bitterly hated; the natives will not tolerate one of them, but look upon them as their mortal foes. So, when the sultan of Aden learnt that this bishop was a Christian and an emissary of the great king of Abyssinia, he had him arrested there and then and demanded to know whether he was a Christian. The bishop replied that he was so in very truth. The sultan told him that if he would not profess the faith of Mahomet, he would be put to utter shame and disgrace. The bishop answered that he would sooner be killed than renounce his faith. When the sultan heard this answer, he abused him shamefully and ordered that he should be circumcised. So a band of his men laid hands on him and circumcised him in the fashion of the Saracens. This done, the sultan avowed that this affront had been put upon him in scorn and contempt of the king his master. And with those words he let him go. The bishop was grieved to the heart at the shame he had suffered; but he comforted himself with the thought that he had suffered it for the sake of the Christian faith, and therefore the Lord God would requite his soul in the next world.

Not to make too long a tale of it, you may take it

that, when the bishop was healed and able to ride, he
went on his way with his company. He travelled by sea
and land till he came to Abyssinia to his lord the king.
The king was overjoyed to see him and made him
heartily welcome, and then asked for tidings of the
sepulchre. The bishop told him the whole truth about
it, and the king accounted it a holy matter and reposed
great faith in it. Next he reported how the sultan of
Aden had had him circumcised as a mark of scorn and
contempt for his master. When the king heard how
his bishop had been put to shame in contempt of
himself, he was so angry that he came near to dying.
In a voice that all those about him could plainly hear
he vowed that he would neither wear his crown nor
rule his realm if he did not wreak such vengeance
that all the world would speak of it. Be well assured,
therefore, that he mustered a great force of horsemen
and footmen and elephants bearing stoutly fortified
castles manned by fully a score of men apiece. When
all his force was arrayed, he set out on his way and
came to the kingdom of Aden. And the kings of that
province marched out with a great host of Saracens,
both horse and foot, to repel the invasion and took up
a strong position in a pass. When the Abyssinians
reached this pass and found it defended in force, a
bloody battle began. But the upshot was that the kings
of the Saracens, who were three in number, could
not withstand the onslaught of the king of Abyssinia,
whose troops were not deficient either in numbers or
in prowess. For Christians are far more valiant than
Saracens. The Saracens were forced to retreat, and the

Christian monarch with his men entered the kingdom of Aden. Be well assured that in this pass a great multitude of Saracens met their death. What more need I say? Suffice it that at three or four strong positions the Saracens opposed the advance of the Abyssinians into the kingdom of Aden; but all their efforts went for nothing, and vast quantities of them were killed. When the king of the Christians had spent about a month in the territory of his enemies, causing great havoc and destruction and killing great numbers of Saracens, he declared that now the insult to his bishop was well avenged and they could return with honour to their own country. Besides, he could do no further damage to the enemy, because he would have to traverse passes of great strength in which a few defenders could inflict heavy losses. So the Christians withdrew from the kingdom of Aden and did not stop till they had reached their own land of Abyssinia. And now you have heard how well and amply the bishop was avenged on these Saracen dogs. For the numbers killed were almost past counting, not to speak of all the lands that were ravaged and laid waste. And no wonder; for it is not fitting that Saracen dogs should lord it over Christians.

Now let us pass on and tell you more about the province of Abyssinia itself. You may take it for a fact that this province is bountifully supplied with all the means of life. The people live on rice, wheat, meat, milk, and sesame. They have elephants; but these are not native to the country but imported from the islands of the other Indies. But giraffes are native and plentiful.

Lions, leopards, and lynxes abound, and a multitude of other beasts different from those of our countries. There are also wild asses in plenty and birds of many sorts unlike those found elsewhere. They have the prettiest hens to be seen anywhere, and enormous ostriches scarcely smaller than a donkey. In short the diversity of animals is such that it would be tedious to enumerate them. But you may be well assured that they have no lack of game, whether beast or bird. They have gaily coloured parrots and monkeys of many sorts, including 'Paul cats' and 'Maimon cats' of such distinctive appearance that some of them can almost be said to have the faces of men.

Finally, let me add that Abyssinia has many cities and towns and the population includes a class of merchants living by trade. Good cotton and buckram cloths are woven here. There is much else that might be told, but it cannot claim a place in our book. So we shall go on now to speak of Aden.

In Aden there is a lord who goes by the title of sultan. The people are all Saracens who worship Mahomet and bear no good will towards Christians. There are many cities and towns. Aden itself is the port to which all the ships from India come with their merchandise. It is a great resort of merchants. In this port they transfer their goods to other small ships, which sail for seven days along a river. At the end of this time they unload the goods and pack them on camels and carry them thus for about thirty days, after which they reach the river of Alexandria; and down this river they are easily transported to Alexandria itself. This is the route from Aden by which the Saracens of Alexandria receive pepper and spices and precious wares; and there is no other route as easy and as short as this.

Aden is also the starting point for many merchant ships sailing to the Indies. From it they export to India many fine Arab chargers, on which they make a handsome profit. For I would have you know that they sell a good horse in India for 100 marks of silver and more. And I assure you that the sultan of Aden derives a very large revenue from the heavy duties he levies from the merchants coming and going in his country. Indeed, thanks to these, he is one of the richest rulers in the world.

Let me tell you of one thing this sultan did that inflicted a heavy blow on the Christians. For you must know that, when the sultan of Egypt marched against the town of Acre and captured it, to the great loss of the Christians, this sultan of Aden contributed to his forces fully 30,000 horsemen and 40,000 camels, much to the advantage of the Saracens and the detriment of the Christians. And this he did more from ill will to the Christians than from any good will to the sultan of Egypt or from any love he bears him.

We would have you know that the ships of Aden, Hormuz, Kais, and elsewhere that sail on the Indian Ocean are often wrecked because of their frailty. If the sea there were as rough and boisterous as in our parts and as often racked by storms, not a vessel would ever complete her voyage without suffering shipwreck. But what do you think the merchants do, and the seamen who man these craft? They carry with them a number of air-tight skin bags. When tempest threatens and the seas run high, they load these bags with pearls and precious stones, if they have any, and with their clothes and a supply of essential foodstuffs and then they lash them all together to form a raft or float, so that if the ship founders in the storm they are left on the bags. And then after drifting this way or that before the gale for days on end they are at length driven to shore, no matter how far out they may be – even as much as 200 miles. When they are at sea on these rafts, every time they want to eat or drink they take supplies from the bags, which they afterwards inflate by blowing. In this way they escape. But the ships with the bulky merchandise are lost.

Let us go on now to tell of a large city which forms part of the province of Aden but has a petty ruler of its own. This city, which lies about 400 miles north-west of the port of Aden, is called Shihr. It is ruled by a count, who maintains strict justice in his domain. He has several cities and towns under his sway but is himself subject to the sultan of Aden. The people are Saracens and worship Mahomet. The city has a very good port; for I assure you that many merchant-ships come here well loaded with goods from India, and from here they export many goods to India. In particular they export innumerable fine chargers and sturdy pack-horses of great worth and price, on which the merchants make a handsome profit.

This province produces great quantities of excellent

white incense, and also dates in great abundance. No grain is grown here except rice, and not much of that; but it is imported from abroad at a big profit. Fish is plentiful, notably tunnies of large size, which are so abundant that two of them can be bought for a Venetian groat. The staple diet consists of rice, meat, and fish. They have no grape wine, but make a wine of sugar, rice, and dates. And let me tell you something else. They have sheep here that have no ears, nor even ear-holes; but in the place where ears ought to be they have little horns. They are small creatures and very pretty. And here is something else that may strike you as marvellous: their domestic animals — sheep, oxen, camels, and little ponies — are fed on fish. They are reduced to this diet because in all this country and in all the surrounding regions there is no grass; but it is the driest place in the world. The fish on which these animals feed are very small and are caught in March, April, and May in quantities that are truly amazing. They are then dried and stored in the houses and given to the animals as food throughout the year. I can tell you further that the animals also eat them alive, as soon as they are drawn out of the water. There are also big fish here — and good ones too — in great profusion and very cheap. They even make biscuit out of fish. They chop a pound or so of fish into little morsels and dry it in the sun and then store it in their houses and eat it all the year round like biscuit. As for the incense of which I have spoken, which grows here in such profusion, the lord buys it for 10 gold bezants a *cantar* and then sells it to foreign merchants and others for

40 bezants a *cantar*. The lord of Shihr does this on behalf of the sultan of the province of Aden. For the sultan of Aden has incense bought up throughout his dominions at the price of 10 bezants and afterwards sold at 40, from which he derives an immense profit. As there is nothing else here worth mentioning, we shall go on to speak of Dhofar.

Dhofar is a fine city of great size and splendour lying about 500 miles north-west of Shihr. Here again the people are Saracens and worship Mahomet, and are subject to a count who is likewise subject to the sultan of Aden. You must understand that this city is still within the province of Aden. The city stands on the sea and has a very good port, frequented by many merchant ships that import and export great quantities of merchandise. Many good Arab steeds, and horses from other lands as well, are brought here, and the merchants make a handsome profit on them. The city has many other cities and towns under its sway. Here again good incense grows in profusion – I will tell you how. It is produced by trees of no great size, like little fir trees. They are gashed with knives in various places, and out of these gashes oozes the incense. Some of it even oozes from the tree itself without any gashing, in consequence of the great heat that prevails. As for the Arab steeds that are brought here, the merchants afterwards export them to India, making a good profit on the deal. As there is nothing else worth mentioning, we shall go on to tell of the gulf of Kalhat.

*

Kalhat is a large city lying inside the gulf which is also called Kalhat. It is a fine city on the sea-coast 600 miles north-west of Dhofar. The people are Saracens who worship Mahomet. They are subject to Hormuz; and whenever the *malik* of Hormuz is at war with neighbours more powerful than himself, he comes to this city, because it is strongly built and situated, so that here he is afraid of no one. No corn is grown here, but it is imported by sea from other places. This city has a very good port, much frequented by merchant ships from India. They find a ready market here for their wares, since it is a centre from which spices and other goods are carried to various inland cities and towns. Many fine war horses are exported from here to India, to the great gain of the merchants. The total number of horses shipped to India from this port and the others I have mentioned is past all reckoning.

The city stands at the mouth or entrance of the gulf of Kalhat, so that no ship can enter or leave the gulf except by leave of its rulers. The *malik* of this city thus has a powerful hold over the sultan of Kerman, to whom he is subject. For sometimes the sultan imposes some due on the *malik* of Hormuz or one of his brethren, and they refuse to pay it, and the sultan sends an army to enforce payment. At such times they leave Hormuz and take ship and cross over to Kalhat and stay there and do not let a single ship pass. This means a great loss to the sultan, who is accordingly obliged to make peace with the *malik* and moderate his demands for money. I should add that the *malik* of Hormuz has a castle that is even stronger than this city and commands the gulf and the sea even more effectively.

You may take it for a fact that the people of this country live on dates and salt fish, of which they enjoy abundant supplies. But admittedly there are some among them, men of wealth and consequence, who eat foods of better quality.

Now that we have told you all about the city of Kalhat and the gulf, we shall go on to tell you of Hormuz.

Hormuz lies about 300 miles north-north-west of Kalhat. A journey of about 500 miles west-north-west of Kalhat brings the traveller to Kais; but let us leave Kais and speak of Hormuz.

Hormuz is a great and splendid city on the sea, governed by a *malik* and with several cities and towns in subjection to it. The people are Saracens who worship Mahomet. The climate is excessively hot – so hot that the houses are fitted with ventilators to catch the wind. The ventilators are set to face the quarter from which the wind blows and let it blow into the house. This they do because they cannot endure the over powering heat. But no more of this now, because we told you earlier in the book about Hormuz and Kais and Kerman. Since we went out by another route, it is fitting that we should return to this point.

[...]

Epilogue

You have heard all the facts about Tartars and Saracens as far as they can be told, and about their customs, and about the other countries of the world as far as they can be explored and known, except that we have not spoken to you of the Black Sea or the provinces that lie around it, although we ourselves have explored it thoroughly. I refrain from telling you this, because it seems to me that it would be tedious to recount what is neither needful nor useful and what is daily recounted by others. For there are so many who explore these waters and sail upon them every day – Venetians, Genoese, Pisans and many others who are constantly making this voyage – that everybody knows what is to be found there. Therefore I say nothing on this topic. For our part, as to how we took leave of the Great Khan, you have heard in the prologue to this book, in the chapter that tells of the troubles encountered by Messer Maffeo and Messer Niccolò and Messer Marco in getting his leave to depart and of the happy chance that led to our departure. And you must know that, but for this chance, we might never have got away for all our pains, so that there is little likelihood that we should ever have returned to our own country. But I believe it was God's will that we should return, so that men might know the things that are in the world, since, as we have said in the first chapter of this book, there was never man yet, Christian or Saracen, Tartar or Pagan, who explored so much of the world as Messer Marco, son of Messer Niccolò Polo, great and noble citizen of the city of Venice.

THANKS BE TO GOD
AMEN AMEN

THE STORY OF PENGUIN CLASSICS

Before 1946 …'Classics' are mainly the domain of academics and students, without readable editions for everyone else. This all changes when a little-known classicist, E. V. Rieu, presents Penguin founder Allen Lane with the translation of Homer's *Odyssey* that he has been working on and reading to his wife Nelly in his spare time.

1946 *The Odyssey* becomes the first Penguin Classic published, and promptly sells three million copies. Suddenly, classic books are no longer for the privileged few.

1950s Rieu, now series editor, turns to professional writers for the best modern, readable translations, including Dorothy L. Sayers's *Inferno* and Robert Graves's *The Twelve Caesars*, which revives the salacious original.

1960s The Classics are given the distinctive black jackets that have remained a constant throughout the series's various looks. Rieu retires in 1964, hailing the Penguin Classics list as 'the greatest educative force of the 20th century'.

1970s A new generation of translators arrives to swell the Penguin Classics ranks, and the list grows to encompass more philosophy, religion, science, history and politics.

1980s The Penguin American Library joins the Classics stable, with titles such as *The Last of the Mohicans* safeguarded. Penguin Classics now offers the most comprehensive library of world literature available.

1990s The launch of Penguin Audiobooks brings the classics to a listening audience for the first time, and in 1999 the launch of the Penguin Classics website takes them online to a larger global readership than ever before.

The 21st Century Penguin Classics are rejacketed for the first time in nearly twenty years. This world famous series now consists of more than 1300 titles, making the widest range of the best books ever written available to millions – and constantly redefining the meaning of what makes a 'classic'.

The Odyssey continues …

The best books ever written

PENGUIN ⦿ CLASSICS

SINCE 1946

Find out more at www.penguinclassics.com